Pandemic Press Media Magazine

Fall/Autumn 2022 Volume 1, Issue 2

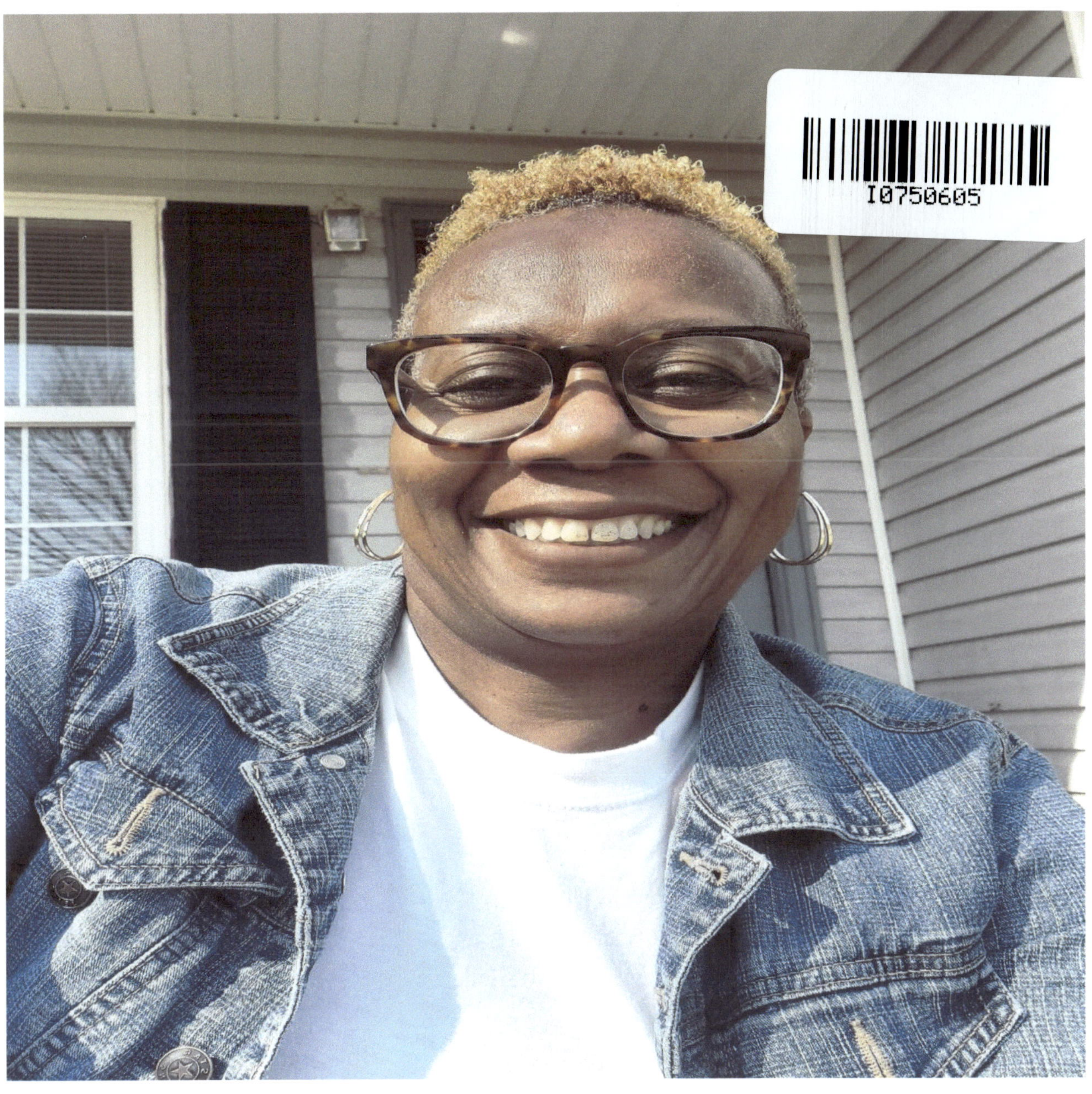

Inside This Issue:

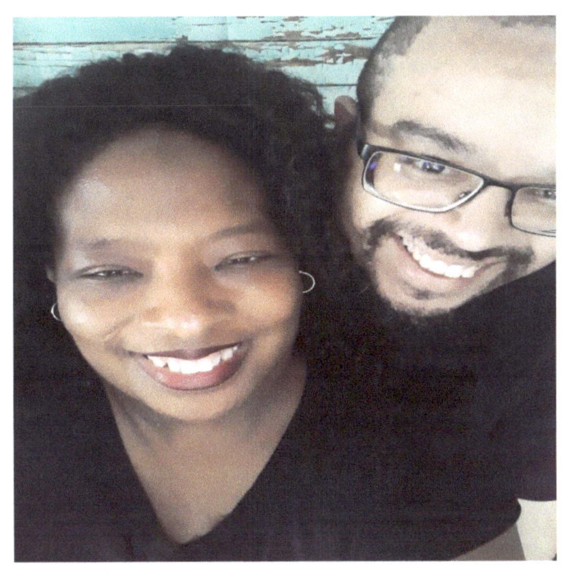

Letter From The Editors

Welcome back to Pandemic Press Media Magazine- a cultural and lifestyle magazine!! Brought to you by Pandemic Press Media, LLC! Thank you for joining us for the Fall/Autumn Edition! (This magazine is a quarterly publication.)

We are dedicated to bringing you the best information, cover stories, feature stories, reviews, music, sports and more! We will also begin tapping into the lives of positive, industry leaders!

We have so much going on in this magazine this month, that we didn't think that there would be enough paper to contain it! Glide through the pages and let us know what you think!

Also, if there is something that we aren't reporting that you would like to see, please let us know!

Sincerely,

Samuel and Bobbie Cubbage

Cover Story

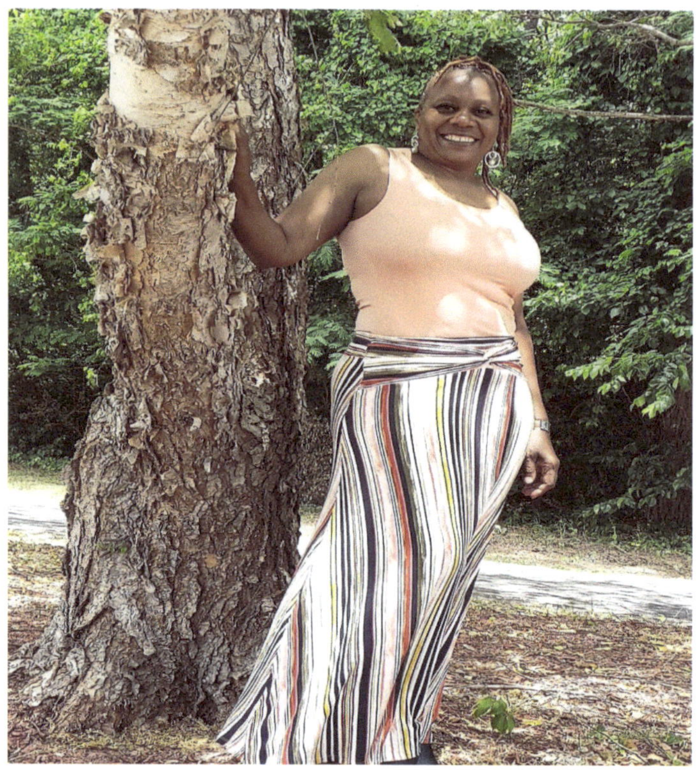

One on One with Ramona Dixon

PPM Magazine– Our guest today is the author of a book called, "Better Days are Coming". Let's welcome, Ramona Dixon! Welcome Ramona! We are really happy to have you here.

RD– Thank you for having me! I appreciate it. I'm so happy that you guys invited me in. So, thank you. I feel good. I feel ready.

PPM Magazine– Absolutely! We had to roll out the red carpet! We heard about you and your story from a mutual friend and fellow author, Enda Jones. And speaking of writing, have you ever thought about collaborating with any other authors?

RD-Only Enda. Enda Jones. We've talked and she's helped me out a lot. Actually, she's one that told me about you all. I appreciate her and shout out to her.

PPM Magazine– We had the opportunity to read your book. And it's so inspiring! It really grasps at your heart. Can you tell our audience a little bit about yourself?

RD– Sure! I always start out by telling people that I'm an old, country girl, raised on a farm in the country- of Cotton Plant, Arkansas. A very small town. But, I love it. I LOVE it! That's where I received all of my good morals and ethics; and how to live a good life. I'm one of 7 children to my parents- who have gone on to glory. I have one beautiful daughter. I love her very, very much! She's 21 years old. Doing exceedingly well. Shoutout to her! I dedicated this book on her behalf. Monet is my daughter's middle name. That's where the book title, (the author), comes from. I'm just excited today! I'm still in the process of healing. It's an ongoing process. It never ends. I'm just excited. It's an exciting day for me!

PPM Magazine-We are so happy that you told us about the Monet at the top of the book. We did a little digging and found some great reviews of the book. Then we saw that Monet was your daughter's middle name- that makes sense. Thank you for clearing that up for us! Did It take you a long time to get this book written?

RD- Yes, it did! People kept telling me that I need to write a book and that my story needs to be heard. A lot of people need to hear what you've gone through. It's reality. I just didn't see myself being an author and writing. I figured, " I don't have the time to write a book." But God sat me down and said that I needed to write.

PPM Magazine: Is there any situation in the book that you would like to discuss?

RD-One of the biggest things is that a marriage is two people. It has nothing to do with a third party. That's what those rings are for. Those rings are a circle. The ring doesn't have a split. But if it does have a split, then it's time to find out why we have a split in this ring. I remember the pastor that married me at that time explained to us what that meant. That's a seal; and we were grounded before God.

PPM Magazine-It's so nice to see all of the love and support of the people who have supported you and your book.

RD-I am very grateful for my friends and family.

PPM Magazine– How did you hold on to faith?

RD- CLC Worldwide Ministries in Rex, GA. Pastor Karl Miller. He has GREAT teachings. I've learned a lot through him; through his teachings. Sometimes I would go to church, it seemed like he knew what sermon to speak on. And it was like he was talking to me. I've always been told that when you go to church and the sermon falls on you, you feel like, "Oh! Is he talking to me?" That's the Holy Spirit working on you.

PPM Magazine- What would you say to someone who is going through these same struggles as you have?

RD- Hang in there. God hears you; He's going to bottle up your tears. And He's going to get you through it.

PPM Magazine- We really appreciate you speaking with us.

RD- Yes, Thank you all so much for your support! I love you all! Please share the story and share the book! Get it for someone else if they need it. I just thank you guys so much!

PPM Magazine- Thank you so much and we definitely want to have you come back when you can!

RD- I appreciate it! Thank you so much!

Cooking Fun with Mrs. Cubbage!!

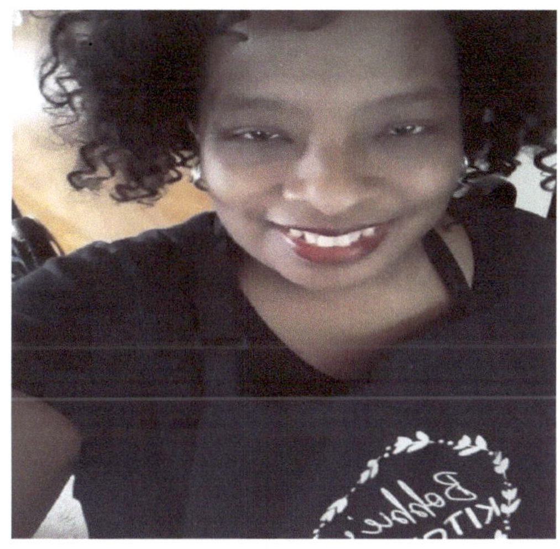

Hellooooooo, Everybody!! I'm so happy to have you here! I'm Mrs. Cubbage! I am an author, early childhood educator, wife, daughter, sister, friend, podcaster, certified life coach and entrepreneur! One thing I love doing is teaching! Teaching people. Especially young people. One thing that I really enjoy is teaching young people how to cook. Once they master that skill; along with gaining the confidence to excel in the kitchen, everything else that they try to do is easy! New episodes of my show are available Fridays at 4PM EST on The CCI Radio Show YouTube Channel!

Here are a few recipes from my book, “Cooking Fun with Mrs. Cubbage” that you and your family are sure to LOVE!

Over the years, one thing I learned is that the children are NOT interested in ACTUALLY learning about what each kitchen utensil can do; they are ready to get messy, and EAT! This particular recipe is SOOOO easy! But, if you do not assign enough jobs for/to the children, you are going to have a lot of little people asking, “What’s next? What can I do? Can I do what he’s doing?” So, break up the instructions and ingredients into as many children that you have. That will slow down (not stop) the many questions that are sure to come your way.

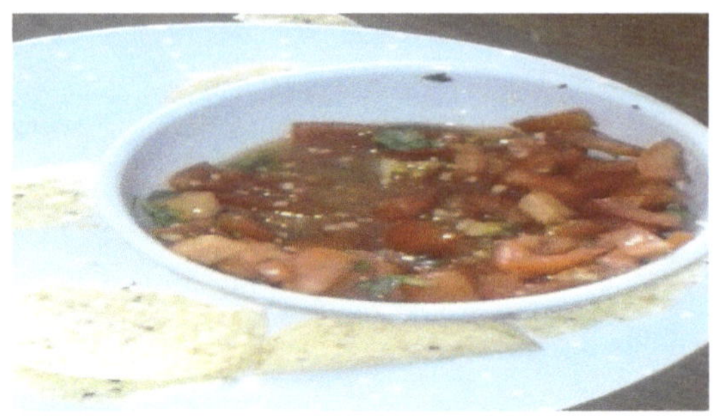

Easy Homemade Salsa

Ingredients

- Fresh tomatoes – use the nice, red ones, avoid anything soft.
- Fresh cilantro – cilantro adds a nice flavor.
- Yellow onion- green onion can be used here, as well.
- Garlic
- Lime – gives the salsa a boost!
- Chili powder
- Sugar – just a pinch. It helps to balance the acidity of the tomatoes and lime.
- Salt and pepper – to taste

Directions

Chop ALL of the vegetables, and put them into a large bowl. Combine garlic, onion, 1/2 teaspoon salt, and 1/4 teaspoon pepper. Add the tomatoes, lime juice, and oil and toss to combine. Fold in the cilantro. Put in the refrigerator for 30 minutes. Grab your favorite bag of tortilla chips! Enjoy!

Spanakopita

Ingredients

- 3 tablespoons olive oil
- 1 large onion, chopped
- 2 cloves garlic, minced
- 2 pounds spinach, rinsed and chopped
- 1/2 cup chopped fresh parsley (Preferred)
- 2 eggs, lightly beaten
- 1/2 cup ricotta cheese
- 1 cup crumbled feta cheese
- 8 sheets phyllo dough

Directions

1. Preheat the oven to 350 degrees F. Lightly oil a 9x9 inch square baking pan.
2. Heat 3 tablespoons of olive oil in a large skillet over medium heat. Saute onion, green onions and garlic, until soft and golden brown. Stir in spinach and parsley, and continue to saute until spinach is soft, about 2 minutes. Remove from heat and set aside.
3. In a medium bowl, mix together eggs, ricotta, and feta. Stir in spinach mixture. Lay 1 sheet of phyllo dough in a prepared baking pan, and brush lightly with olive oil. Lay another sheet of phyllo dough on top, brush with olive oil, and repeat the process with two more sheets of phyllo. The sheets will overlap the pan. Spread spinach and cheese mixture into pan and fold overhanging dough over filling. Brush with oil, then layer remaining 4 sheets of phyllo dough, brushing each with oil. Tuck in the overhanging dough into the pan to seal the filling.
4. Bake in a preheated oven for 35 minutes. Or, until golden brown. Cut into squares; usually you would serve it hot. But, with the children, wait for a little while, and then serve.

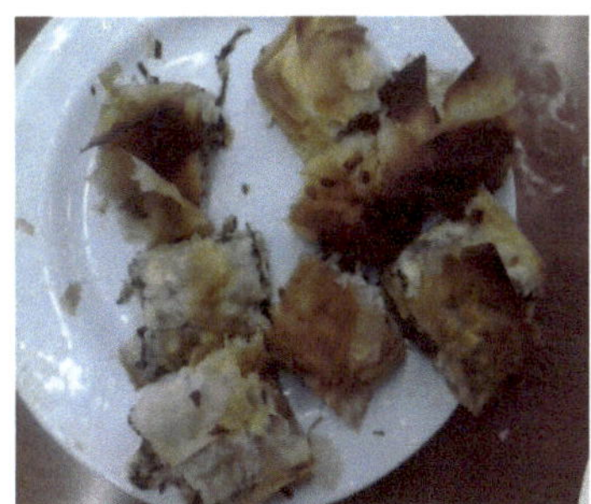

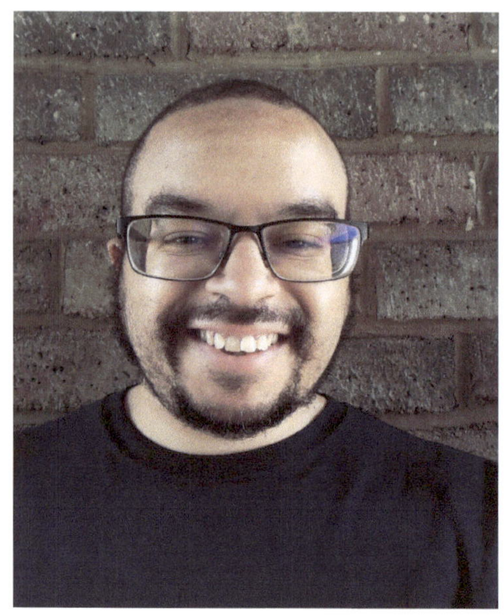

The Music Spotlight w/ Sam C. Smooth

Welcome to this edition of The Music Spotlight with Sam C. Smooth! I will give you the latest music news along with my own "Top 10" Albums and Singles of the Fall from my favorite music genres. Let's get started!

Latest music news:

The music world suffered a great loss on August 8th of this year. Olivia Newton John, singer, actress and activist, passed away. She left a legacy of wonderful songs and movies. Of course, one of my favorites, along with her performance as Sandy in Grease were her films Xanadu and One Of A Kind! She will truly be missed! And now, here are my picks for favorite singles and albums per genre for this edition of our magazine!

Sam C's Top 10 80's Albums

1. George Michael-Faith

2. Janet Jackson- Control

3. Peter Gabriel- So

4. Prince-Sign O' The Times

5. Guns N' Roses- Appetite For Destruction

6. Lionel Richie- Can't Slow Down

7. Gladys Knight And The Pips- All Our Love

8. Alexander O'Neal-Hearsay

9. Rick James-Street Songs

10. The SOS Band- On The Rise

Sam C's Top 10 80's Singles

1. Never Gonna Give You Up-Rick Astley

2. Genius Of Love-Tom Tom Club

3. Kiss- Prince And The Revolution

4. Buffalo Stance-Neneh Cherry

5, West End Girls- Pet Shop Boys

6. Don't You (Forget About Me)- Simple Minds

7. Tainted Love-Soft Cell

8. Relax- Frankie Goes To Hollywood

9. Superfreak- Rick James

10. Everybody Wants To Rule The World-Tears For Fears

Sam C's Top 70's Albums

1. ABC-The Jacksons

2. Rumours- Fleetwood Mac

3. Hotel California- The Eagles

4. News Of The World- Queen

5. Arrival- ABBA

6. Off The Wall- Michael Jackson

6. Miss Gladys Knight- Gladys Knight

7. Jolene- Dolly Parton

8. GoodBye Yellow Brick Road- Elton John

9. Atlantic Crossing- Rod Stewart

10. Storm At Sunup- Gino Vannelli

Sam C's Top 70's Singles

1. Bohemian Rhapsody- Queen

2. Heart Of Glass- Blondie

3. Imagine-John Lennon

4. Could It Be I'm Falling In Love- The Spinners

5. Tiny Dancer-Elton John

6. I'll Be There- The Jacksons

7. Tears Of A Clown- Smokey Robinson And The Miracles

8. I Honestly Love You- Olivia Newton John

9. Kung Fu Fighting-Carl Douglas

10. Let's Do It Again- The Staple Singers

Sam C's Top 10 60's Albums

1. Green Onions- Booker T And The MG's
2. I Heard It Through The Grapevine-Marvin Gaye
3. Howlin' Wolf- Howlin' Wolf
4. Lady Soul- Aretha Franklin
5. At Last- Etta James
6. Night Beat- Sam Cooke
7. In A Silent Way- Miles Davis
8. Otis Blue- Otis Redding
9. Stand- Sly And The Family Stone
10. A Long Supreme- John Coltrane

Sam C's Top 10 60's Singles

1. I Can't Stop Loving You- Ray Charles
2. The Twist- Chubby Checker
3. I'm Sorry- Brenda Lee
4. Big Girls Don't Cry- The Four Seasons
5. I'm A Believer- The Monkees
6. Sugar, Sugar- The Archies
7. Hello Dolly- Louis Armstrong And The All Stars
8. Big Bad John- Jimmy Dean
9. Tossin' And Turnin'- Bobby Lewis
10. I Want To Hold Your Hand- The Beatles

Sam C's Top 10 Gospel Albums

1. Joy In The Morning- Tauren Wells

2. All Things New- Tye Tribett

3. Heart, Passion, Pursuit- Tasha Cobbs Leonard

4. Reason To Smile- Kojey Radical

5. Seven- Brooke Frasier

6. Kumama- Grace Lokwa

7. We Are Fire- TY Bello

8. Kingdom Book One- Kirk Franklin

9. Overflow- Frank Edwards

10. Names Of God- Nathaniel Bassey

Sam C's Top 10 Gospel Singles

1. Let Him In- Jokia

2. Never Lost-Cece Winans

3. I'll Go- Jermaine Dolly

4. I Can't Give Up- Byron Cage

5. Lifted Up- VaShawn Mitchell

6. Repay You- PJ Morton and J Moss

7. Grace- Jonathan McReynolds

8. I'm Not Ashamed- Monica Lisa Stevenson

9. Wait-Nia Allen

10. In Jesus Name- Bebe Winans

Sam C's Top 10 Soundtrack Albums

1. Purple Rain
2. Grease
3. Saturday Night Fever
4. Waiting To Exhale
5. Titanic
6. Top Gun
7. The Sound Of Music
8. The Bodyguard
9. Pretty In Pink
10. 8 Mile

Sam C's Top 10 Smooth Jazz Albums

1. Breezin'- George Benson
2. Winelight-Grover Washington, Jr
3. Breakin' Away- Al Jarreau
4. Share My World- Najee
5. Breathless- Kenny G
6. Rites Of Summer- Spyro Gyra
7. Double Vision- David Sanborn
8. Salt- Lizz Wright
9. Three- Bob James
10. Magic Touch- Stanley Jordan

Sam C's Top 10 Smooth Jazz Singles

1. Affirmation- George Benson

2. Since I Fell For You- Bob James

3. Rainbows Of Love- Lonnie Liston Smith

4. Incognito- Deep Water

5. Your Love Is King- Sade

6. 6295 SW Fisher-George Shaw

7. Sade- Kenny G

8. Good Morning Heartache- Chris Botti F/ Jill Scott

9. Winelight- Grover Washington, Jr

10. Dr. Norm-Dave Koz

Sam C's Top 10 Disco Albums

1. The Boss- Diana Ross

2. Off The Wall- Michael Jackson

3. Step II- Sylvester

4. I Am- Earth, Wind and Fire

5. We Are Family- Sister Sledge

6. Never Can Say Goodbye- Gloria Gaynor

7. Portfolio- Grace Jones

8. Triumph- The Jacksons

9. The Glow Of Love- Change

10. C'est Chic- Chic

Sam C's Top 10 Disco Singles

1. Night Fever- The Bee Gees
2. Don't Leave Me This Way- Thelma Houston
3. Disco Inferno- The Tramps
4. Last Dance- Donna Summer
5. I Will Survive- Gloria Gaynor
6. Love Hangover- Diana Ross
7. Knock On Wood- Amii Stewart
8. Funkytown- Lipps, Inc
9. Fly, Robin, Fly-Silver Connection
10. The Hustle- Van McCoy

Sam C's Top 10 90's Hip Hop Albums

1. Illmatic-Nas
2. The Low End Theory- A Tribe Called Quest
3. The Chronic- Dr. Dre
4. Doggystyle-Snoop Doggy Dogg
5. Ready To Die-The Notorious BIG
6. Original Gangster- Ice T
7. Step In The Arena- Gangstarr
8. Fear Of A Black Planet- Public Enemy
9. The Infamous-Mobb Deep
10. Me Against The World- 2Pac

Sam C's Top 10 90's Hip Hop Singles

1. They Reminisce Over You- Pete Rock & CL Smooth

2. C.R.E.A.M-Wu-Tang Clan

3. Mind Playing Tricks On Me- Geto Boys

4. Dear Mama- 2Pac

5. Mama Said Knock You Out- LL Cool J

6. Juicy- The Notorious BIG

7. Nuthin' But A G' Thang- Dr. Dre ft/ Snoop Doggy Dogg

8. Love's Gonna Get 'Cha- Boogie Down Productions

9. Regulate- Warren G ft/ Nate Dogg

10. Eric B & Rakim- Know The Ledge

At the Movies

With Bobbie D.

At the start of the pandemic, it was hard to go out to the movies. However, streaming services began to make it easier to view those new movies from home. Now, with things attempting to get back to normal, the theaters are welcoming movie-goers back into their buildings.

In this segment, I am going to review a mix of movies from the past and present. These movie reviews will cover a variety of genres as well. Let's get started!

Today, I am going to review a POPULAR 80's movie!

(Disclaimer: These are my opinions of the movie. If you haven't seen the movie, I will do my best to NOT ruin it for you.)

I am a fan of 1980's SLASHER movies! The main reason is that I know that these things can't happen in 'real life'. For instance, Freddy Kruger. He's my FAVORITE horror film villian! He can get you in your sleep, AND when you are awake! And we KNOW that NO ONE can get you in your dreams. But, I think that's the fun of it. Just to have that JUMP SCARE!

Nightmare on Elm Street (the Original)-- This movie franchise has been a powerhouse since the 1980's! So much so that it has several parts and a remake to it! Many of the other movies in this franchise are pretty good; but, nothing beats the original. If you haven't seen it, check it out! (It must be streaming somewhere! LOL!)

Even though there are movie villains before the 80's, I feel that this movie started a long line of twisted, wild and crazy movies (and television shows!)

If you are under the age of 30 and wonder where it all started, well— here you go!

I hope that you liked my review of the ORIGINAL, “Nightmare on Elm Street”. If there are any movies that you would like for me to review, please let me know.

In the next edition, I will be discussing CHRISTMAS MOVIES!

Take care and see you at the movies!

TLC Advice Column

Welcome to our ADVICE COLUMN. This is a place where letters from the public will be shared; no names, or personal information will be used. And we will answer the letters to the best of our ability.

Dear Sam C. and Bobbie D.,

I was hoping that you could help me with this problem. I've noticed that people are jealous of me. Seriously! I'm not making this up. They are REALLY jealous of me! I just live my life, as I see fit. And those around me ACT like they are happy for me and my accomplishments. But, I found out through other sources, that I am being ostracized behind my back.
I'm 35, dating a great guy, no kids, great job and family. What should I do? I feel uncomfortable around some people because I know that they don't wish me well.

Dear reader,

Thank you for reaching out to us! We are so sorry that you are experiencing this.
First, it appears from your letter that you have a WONDERFUL support system in your family and your mate. Hold on to that; not many people have that.

Second, you should be proud of your accomplishments. There is nothing wrong with being proud of what you have done. No one can toot your horn better than you.

What we would like to ask is the person that you received the information from a reliable source? Can you really trust them? If so, we would suggest that you check in with that person, just to make sure that they understood what was said about you.

We would also like to suggest that if you feel comfortable with confronting any of your 'friends' to see if they know about this; and if so, maybe they can shed some light on why these things are being said about you.

Thank you for writing in! And please keep us posted.

If you need advice and don't know where to turn, reach out to us @ pandemicpm@gmail.com. Please include in the subject line, "TLC Advice".

Thank you for your support. We invite you to follow and connect with our YouTube Channel, The CCI Radio Show. Please like, click, share and subscribe. You can also listen to our secondary shows, The CCI Radio Show "Gospel Excellence w/ The Angel of the Airwaves, Bobbie D" and The CCI Radio Show "Love Notes w/ Sam C Smooth" on Blogtalkradio, Soundcloud, Spotify, Anchor Podcasts and many other social media outlets. Our newest show, The CCI Radio Show "TLC Podcast" is also available on our YouTube Channel!

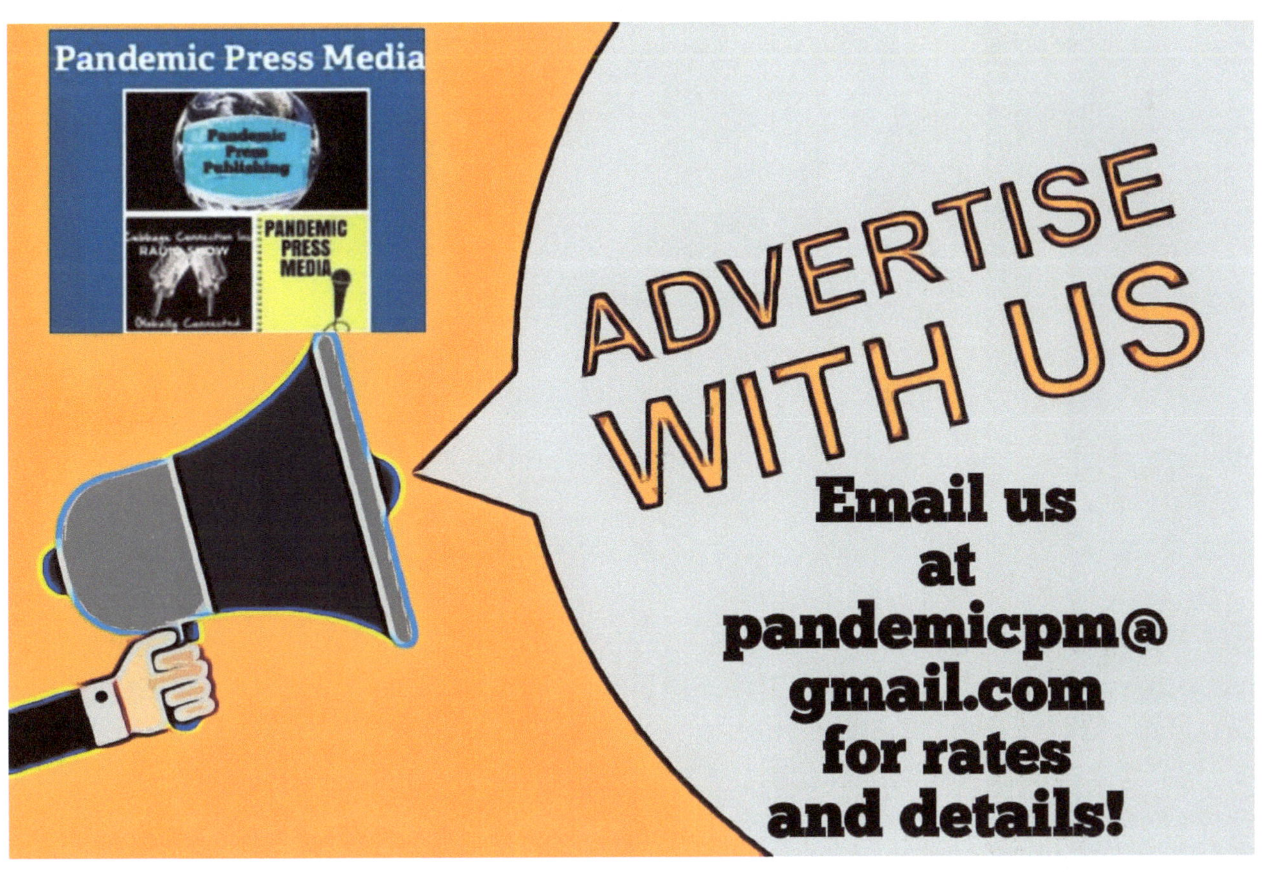

Sam C On Sports

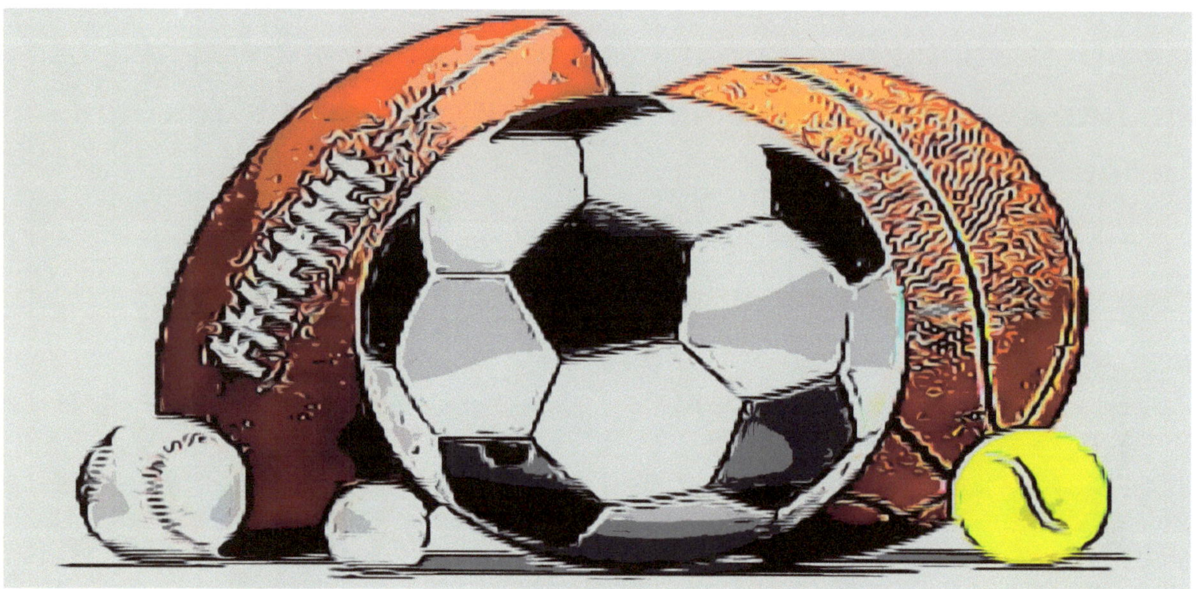

Welcome! This is Sam C On Sports! I will give you the latest sports news and info! Let's get started!

NFL Football: The NFL preseason kicked off not too long ago. It was just a taste to wet our appetite for the start of the real NFL season. I don't know about you but this is my favorite sport. And now, the regular NFL season is underway. So, here we are again. Remember, last season was the first time that the NFL had scheduled a 17 game season for each team. The LA Rams are the current Super Bowl champs. They are ready to defend that title. This should be another great season to watch. Get ready! May the best team win it all! Hopefully, it's one of your teams!

College Football: Here we are at the start of the college football season. I love the passion that college players have. There are some great matchups! Check this out: Pitt Panthers vs. West Virginia Mountaineers in the return of the Backyard Brawl, Florida State Seminoles vs. LSU Tigers and Clemson Tigers vs. Georgia Tech Yellowjackets. These are just some of the great matchups to start the season. The Georgia Bulldogs overcame all of the odds this past season to win the national championship over the Alabama Crimson Tide. Good luck to all the teams!

NBA: The NBA preseason will be underway soon! Some news to provide per multiple sources like ESPN and CBS Sports: Lebron James signed a 2 year deal to remain with the LA Lakers. Can we say it's "Showtime" once again in Los Angeles? We shall see!

NHL: The Hockey preseason will be coming soon! The Colorado Avalanche are the defending Stanley Cup champs! They will be eager to keep that title.

Baseball: We are heading down the homestretch of the regular season! There is still more action to come. Remember, you can watch the MLB on the MLB Network, Peacock Network and Fox Sports!

That's it for now! Thanks for joining me and I'll have more next time!

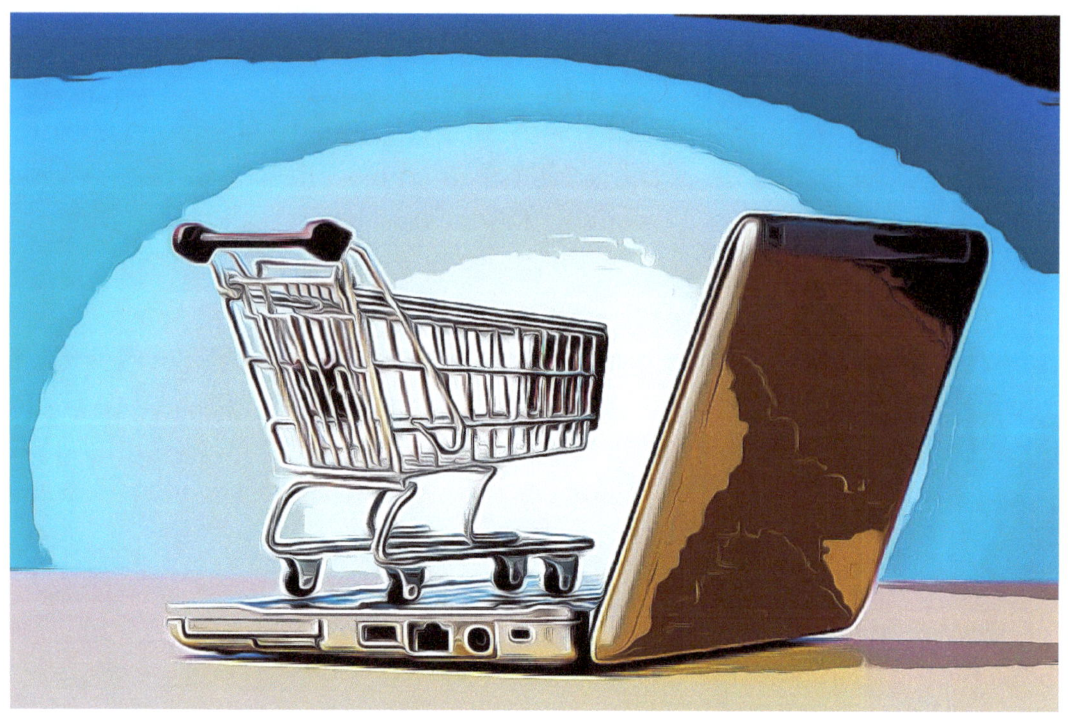

The CUBB House Merch Store

Welcome to The CUBB House Merch Store! This month, we are featuring these following items! Here is this edition's feature item:

"Cooking Fun w/ Mrs. Cubbage" short sleeve T-Shirt in Black w/picture logo

For pricing information and if you would like to see the whole collection line, please visit https://www.pandemicpresspublishing.com/the-cubb-house-merch-store/ !

All items can be paid by CashApp (PandemicPressMedia) or PayPal (Pandemic Press Publishing.) Any questions, please contact Pandemic Press Publishing by emailing pandemicpp@gmail.com!

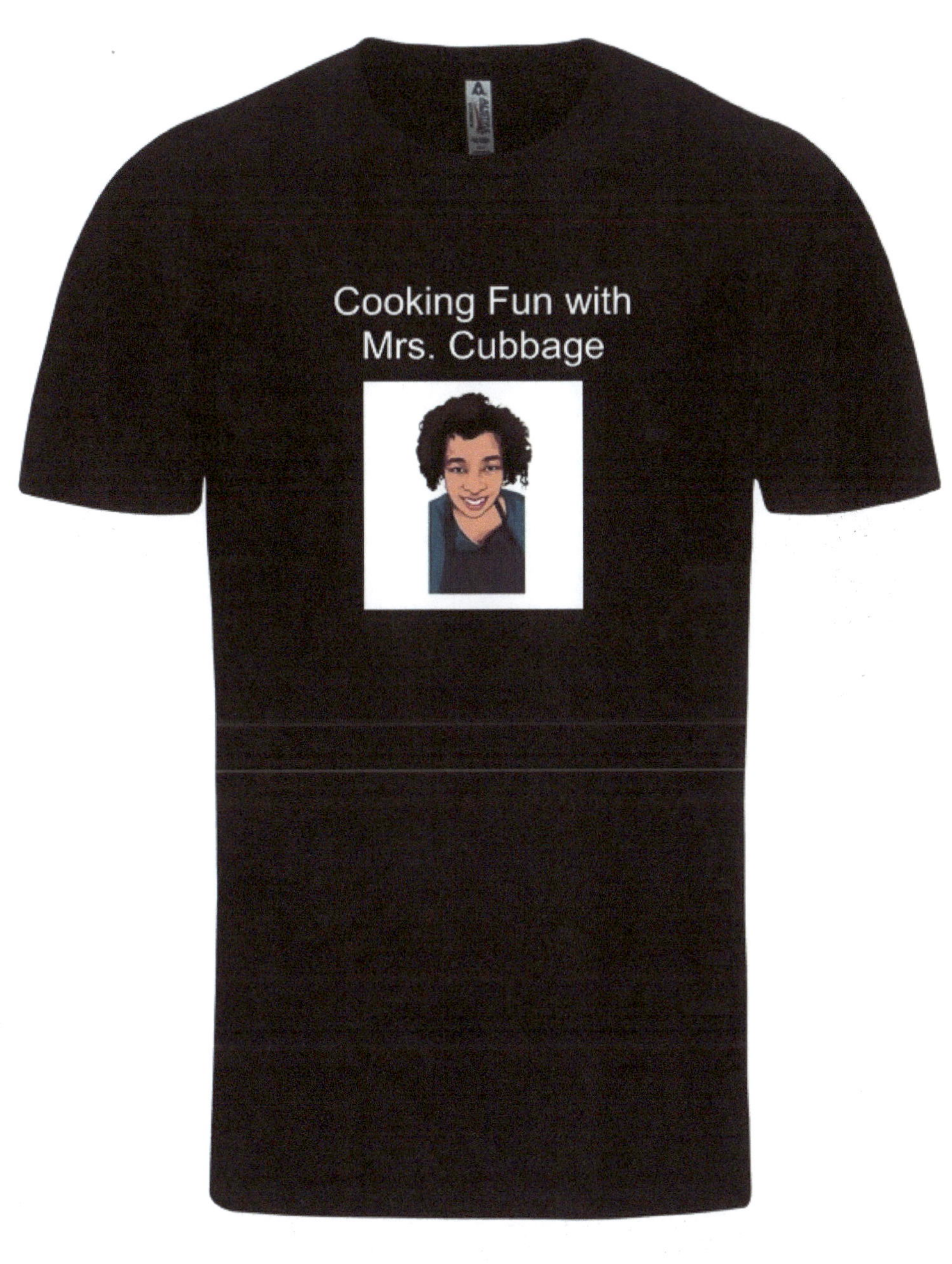
Cooking Fun with
Mrs. Cubbage

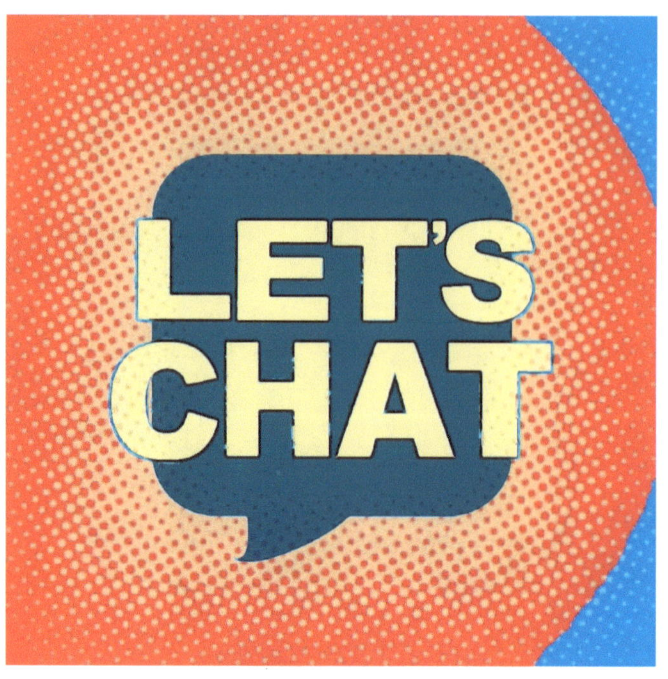

The CUBB House Chat

First: Did you know that The CCI Radio Show celebrated its 10th Anniversary this past January 1st? Yes! We initially started on the Blogtalkradio platform. The show has since branched off into 2 more versions. "Gospel Excellence w/ Bobbie D" is the home of 'The Best Gospel Music and Praise!', and "Love Notes" w/ Sam C Smooth is the home of 'all of your great Slow Jams and Love Songs'. It's "Music For Lovers!"

Each show is done on Sunday. Gospel Excellence is at 10AM EST and Love Notes is at 10PM EST on Blogtalkradio. The shows are also available on Soundcloud, Spotify and Anchor Podcasts soon after! Make sure to find us, especially on Spotify and Anchor Podcasts for any episodes that you may have missed! Currently, we are at Episode #593 on this platform…and climbing!!!

Spotify: https://open.spotify.com/show/0x519bbv8Ysy0OIQFkQpRj
Anchor Podcasts: https://anchor.fm/ccisbglobal
Soundcloud: https://soundcloud.com/ccisbglobal
Blogtalkradio: www.blogtalkradio.com/ccisbglobal

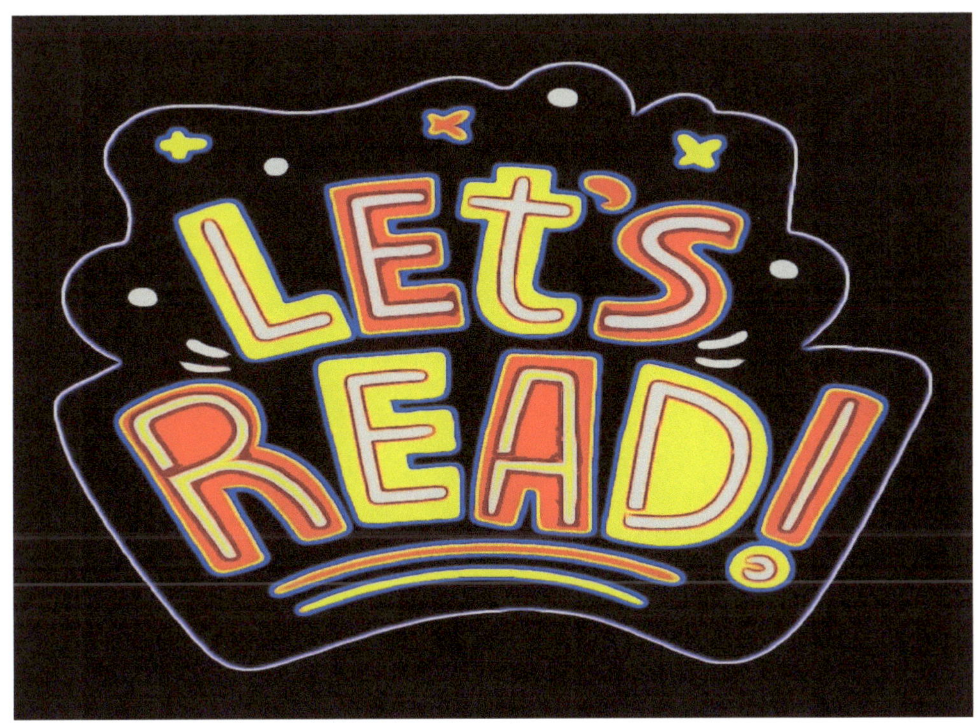

Here is a great book to add to your collection:

I'm Embarrassed to Say, "I was a Gospel Radio DJ!"

A revised version of the original title. Following the ups and downs of being a Gospel Radio DJ, by Bobbie Cubbage.

(Information continued on the next page)...

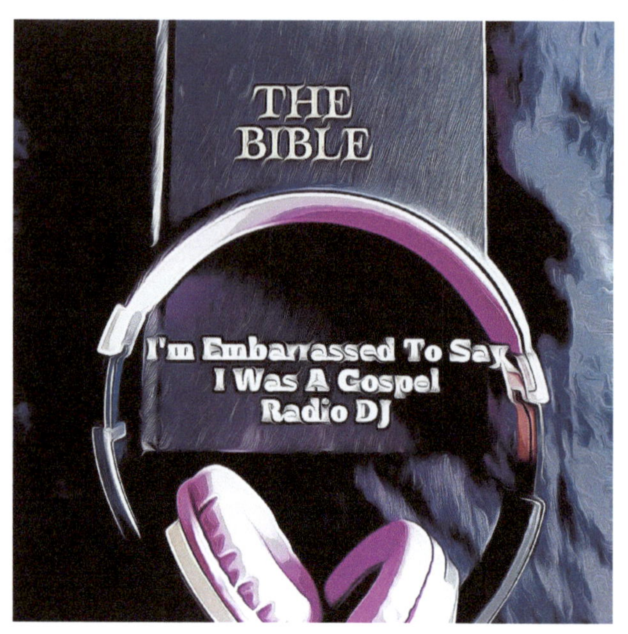

Original book
Publication date 10/23/2003

Revised Publication date
7/24/2022

Available *EXCLUSIVELY* on:

www.lulu.com

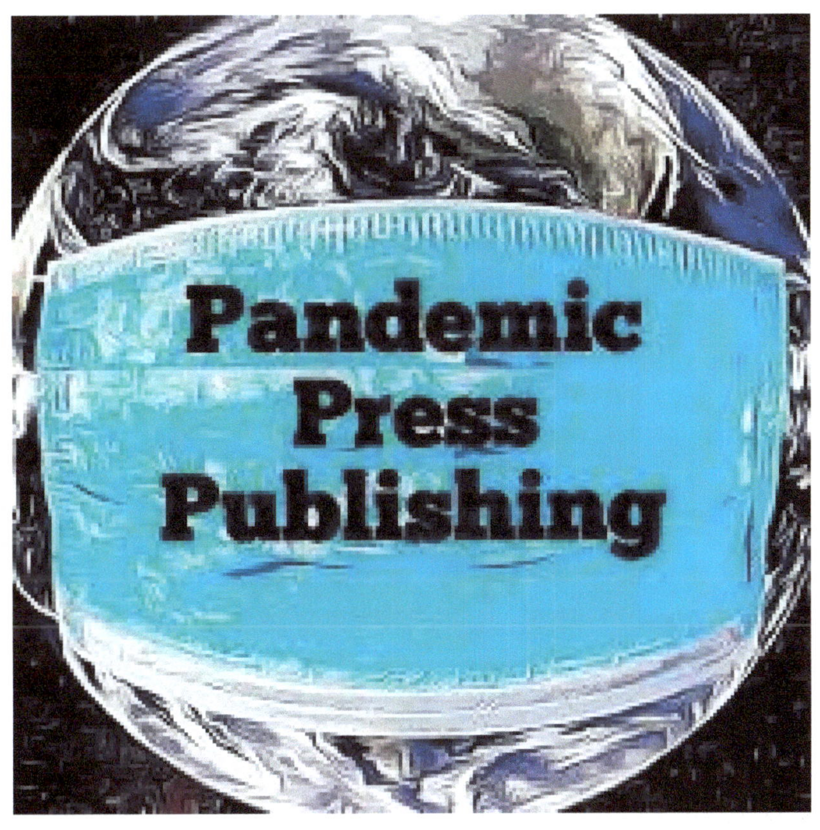
Pandemic
Press
Publishing

Radio Show Spotlight…..

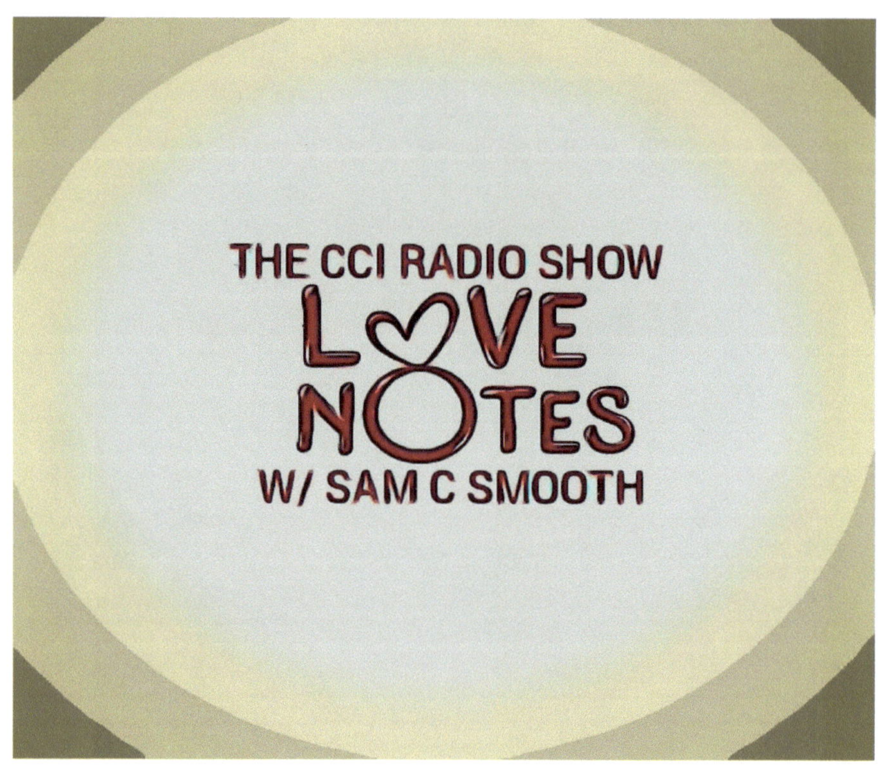

It's music for lovers! Join Sam C. Smooth for great slow jams and love songs! He'll take you to that place and put you in the mood! Tune in 2 Sundays a month at 10pm (EST), on www.blogtalkradio.com, soundcloud, anchor podcasts, spotify, and where podcasts are available!

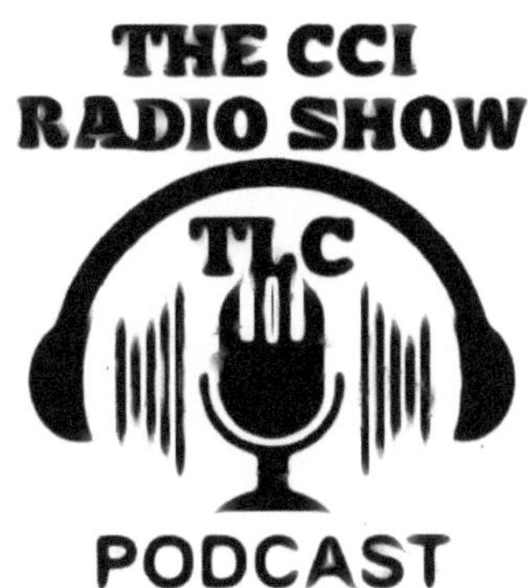

This podcast is the newest edition to The CCI Radio Show programming schedule!It's The CCI Radio Show "TLC Podcast!" It airs every other Saturday morning at 10AM EST on our YouTube Channel, The CCI Radio Show.

Certified Life Coaches, Sam C and Bobbie D want to use this show/platform to help give you some great, useful tips regarding relationships and more.

Tune in LIVE! (If your schedule doesn't permit it, you can ALWAYS go back and watch the show afterwards.)

Please join us!

Are you looking for a little writing inspiration? Do you need some ideas for your "Great American Novel? Look no further than Pandemic Press Publishing's "Writing Inspiration!" Our tips are very informative and worth a try! Lots of tips available! Visit https://www.pandemicpresspublishing.com/ppp-writing-inspiration/ right now!

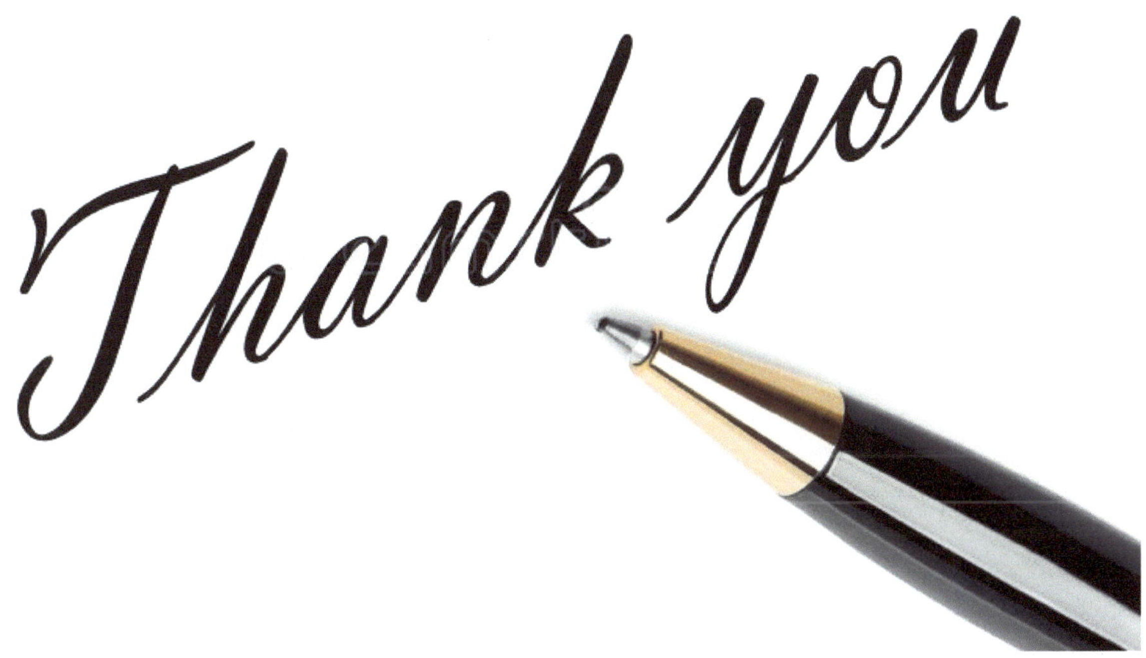

We want to take this time to say "Thank You" for reading this edition of Pandemic Press Media Magazine! (As well as the Summer 2022 edition!) All of your kind words and your continued support is very much appreciated and does not go unnoticed! We look forward to bringing you more great content in our next edition. Stay Tuned!

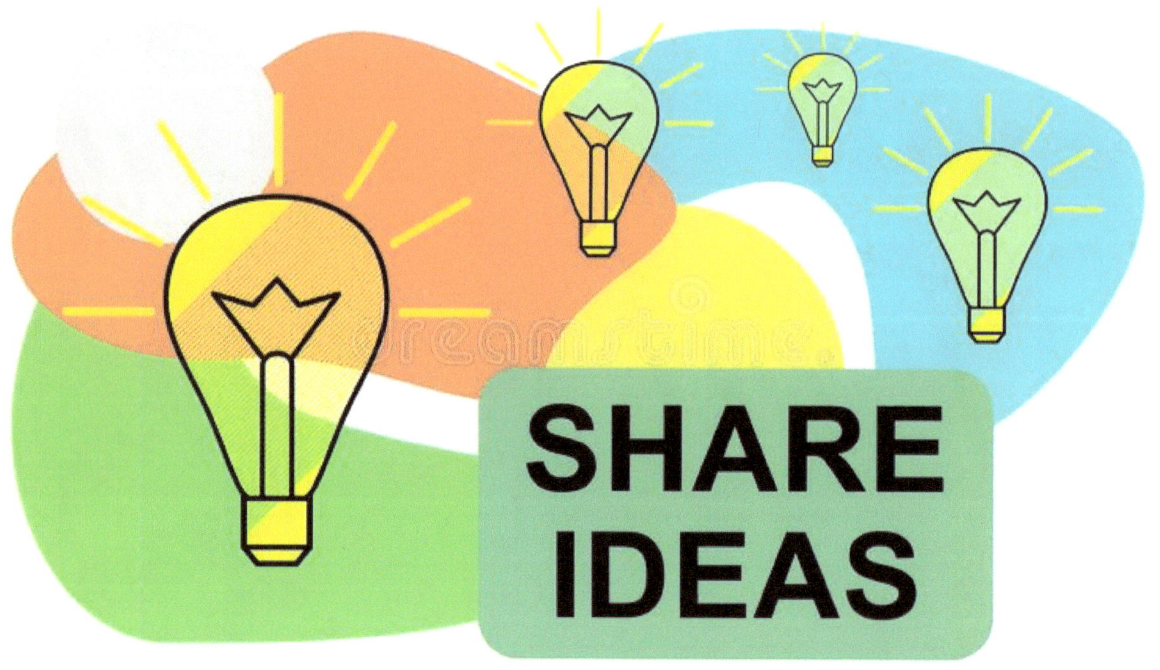

Anything that you would like to see in our magazine? A certain recipe? Do you know someone who would like to be interviewed? Any interesting ideas at all? Let us know and we'll do our best to make it happen!

Samuel and Bobbie Cubbage

Owners/Editors

Pandemic Press Media LLC.

Pittsburgh, PA 15238

www.ingramcontent.com/pod-product-compliance
Lightning Source LLC
LaVergne TN
LVHW070201110826
845147LV00002B/470